Imperfectly
Kind

Imperfectly Kind © 2021 Julie Adam

Edited by Paul Fraumeni

Book Design, cover and interior by Dania Zafar

ISBN: 978-1-7778573-1-8 (paperback)
ISBN: 978-1-7778573-2-5 (hardcover)
ebook ISBN: 978-1-7778573-0-1

Imperfectly *Kind*

Why Kindness Is The Must-Have
Superpower You Need To Lead

JULIE ADAM

To Jack & Cal

CONTENTS

WHY DID I WRITE THIS BOOK?

Throughout my career, I've worked for incredible leaders, been mentored by the best of the best, witnessed brilliance and had the privilege to work alongside the smartest, funniest and most creative people in media. Sure, there have been some duds along the way, but overall, I've been surrounded by excellence. I've won and lost often, have made great decisions and terrible ones and through it all there is one thing that I've learned is more important than anything else in business and life — kindness.

With lockdowns in place for the better part of two years, during the COVID-19 pandemic, I decided to use the extra time on my hands to fulfill a lifelong dream and write this book. It's a collection of my thoughts — 28 of them — on why kindness is the must-have superpower you need to lead. Whether you are a new leader who has just started your first managing gig or a seasoned executive who needs a better approach, I'll show you why kindness works.

I've never aimed for perfection — it's unachievable and not much fun. Instead, I aim for kindness.

Let's get started.

WHY KINDNESS?

People ask me all the time if I always wanted to be in management...run a company...lead a business...be the boss...

The answer is a hard no.

I wanted to be creative! I grew up with a passion for music. It wasn't a pastime, it was a lifeline. I spent hour after hour listening in my room, reading the lyrics, deconstructing the music and the meaning, just getting lost in my dreams of being a musician. I desperately wanted to play in a band, go on the road and write songs. There was only one problem — I have zero musical talent (you either have it or you don't). I switched gears, did a degree in media and quickly fell into radio. I thought I could translate my love of music into being a producer or working on the air hosting a music show. I wasn't exactly sure what I wanted to do other than I was sure I didn't want to be anyone's boss.

As soon as I started working as a teenager, I assumed management was the enemy. They were the people who got in the way of the fun ideas, told you what to do, criticized your work and made you do endless boring jobs. The real reason I didn't want to be in charge was I assumed being a boss meant you had to be a jerk. By definition, a boss is a person who exercises control or authority.

No thanks, I thought, not for me. I was the opposite. I didn't want to discipline anyone or control anything. I wanted to have fun, create things and cause trouble.

What happened? Why did I end up doing the one thing I didn't want to do? And why have I stayed at it for so long?

Two reasons.

People and kindness.

A few years into my career, I learned two pivotal things about myself and my work.

First — the greatest joy for me isn't really about creating something, it is creating something with others. I am not a solo artist. I LOVE people and get charged up when they succeed. Building something with others is the perfect day for me.

Second — you can be the boss and still be kind. This was life-changing because until I realized this, I assumed the only way you could be in charge was if you were prepared to be constantly hard on and mean to people. I knew this style wouldn't work for me, because I knew from early on in life that my one true goal was to try to be a good person.

Turns out that not only is it OK to be kind to people on your team, it is your job to treat them well. We've seen a remarkable transition in leadership over the past two decades. The world has moved away from the screamers and door slammers, the power-hungry lunatics who take joy in humiliating and pushing down others to prop themselves up. No one ever wanted to work for jerks like this, but there was no choice, and people were forced to put up with it. Some companies went along with it, providing the leaders were high performers. That's just how it was.

Over time, technology has changed the business world. The rise of tech has created incredible competition for customers and talent. And this has encouraged people to start quitting their bosses. Their talent is in high demand and they realize they can work for someone who will treat them better. Most people don't quit an organization — they leave their boss. Now, everyone realizes what the smartest leaders already know — if you're good to people, they'll perform better. If you're nice to work with, you'll attract bigger talent. If you're kind to those around you, you'll make people feel good and they'll bring their best work to the table. Top talent, when enabled to be themselves, are the difference between a good business and a great one.

There are many characteristics of a good leader — discipline, integrity, creativity, the ability to think strategically, being a strong negotiator and communicator, self-awareness and vision. You won't meet a strong manager or executive who doesn't have these skills. These are the table stakes needed to manage a business and team. But if you want to transform from good to great and excel in leadership, you need a north star and a superpower to guide you.

Make it kindness.

Practicing kindness in leadership will force you to shift focus away from yourself to the things which matter most — your customers, your employees, your shareholders and your community. It will quash the negativity that stunts growth, innovation, productivity and creativity. Kindness will improve your ability to empathize and help you build trust. When you apply a kindness lens to everything, you look at business problems from a customer's or employee's viewpoint versus your own — and that allows you to see the real issue. Kindness can help you in every single situation. I have never faced a problem where kindness didn't play a role in finding a solution.

On top of all that, being kind makes you feel good. It will boost serotonin and dopamine, which cause your brain to light up and give you a feeling of satisfaction.

This dopamine will also give you the confidence you need to influence and inspire those around you. When your brain is nourished, you can think more clearly and creatively.

There's one other key benefit to leading with kindness — it's contagious. As more leaders use kindness as their north star and superpower, working becomes more rewarding for everyone. Communities thrive with kind leaders looking out for them and pouring resources back into them. Employees who are cared for contribute more to the organization. You will be happier knowing you're competing to win but doing it in a way that makes the world a better place.

Don't get me wrong, I am not a perfect leader. I'm not even sure if I'm a good leader — that is not for me to judge. I don't think you can mark your own homework on your leadership skills. Instead, I focus on what I can control, being true to my north star and leading with kindness.

Throughout the book, I'll share my thoughts and practical tips on why kindness is the most essential trait a leader can have. How it can help you improve your business, team, culture and performance, how kindness can inspire creativity, big ideas and innovation and how leading with kindness can help you be a better person without losing your competitive edge. There is a way to win without being a jerk.

You don't have to be perfect. Perfection is impossible, unrealistic, demotivating and stifling for those around you. You just have to aim to be kind every chance you get.

Be imperfectly kind.

Before we get going, be forewarned there are a lot of baseball analogies in here. I grew up with a Dad and brother who taught me how to read box scores and what a squeeze play is when I was still in kindergarten! Feel free to swap out my nerdy love of the game for something you're passionate about.

CHAPTER 1

KINDNESS + YOU (THE BASICS)

THOUGHT #1: FIRST BE KIND TO YOURSELF

Self-esteem and self-importance are critical to your success. You must value yourself. You must love yourself and you must be kind to yourself.

We all have a voice inside our head who tells us we're not good enough, not smart enough, not strong enough, not rich enough, too old, too young and on and on. I heard podcaster and author Dan Harris describe it as "the voice in my head is an a**hole." We can all talk ourselves out of anything and this type of negativity is destructive.

If you want to be an exceptional leader and are committed to leading with kindness, the first person you need to focus on is yourself. It's like the airplane oxygen mask — before you put the mask on someone else, you put your own on first.

Without self-love, it will be impossible for you to be generous with praise for others or confident in coaching your team if you don't believe in yourself. How will you accept mistakes and failure from others if you won't permit yourself to fail?

How will you guide others to achieve greatness if you think your work is average or worse?

You won't. To help develop greatness in others, you need to be kind and believe in yourself.

Be kind when you fail. Remind yourself that failure is the fastest way to grow and learn. Give yourself permission to make mistakes and hold yourself accountable to learning from them. Remember, kindness isn't only about praise and positivity — true kindness is rooted in honesty and accountability. When you make a mistake, own it, analyze it and move on.

Get over it. So, something went wrong and it's your fault. Develop a short-term memory that allows you to forget the issues of your past and move on. If you continuously beat yourself up, you'll never give yourself permission to get on with things and swing again. The best hitters in baseball get out 70% of the time. Swing, miss, move on and try again.

Be honest about your skillset. What makes you great? Put modesty aside for a moment and write out a list of your skills and accomplishments. Ask yourself, "What is one thing I can do better than most?" This is something to cherish, celebrate and lean on. When you're having a bad day or trying to solve a problem and you're stuck, be kind to yourself. Look back at your list, remind yourself what you're good at and put your skills to work.

Be honest about your weaknesses. What are your blind spots? What is your kryptonite? Where are you wobbly? Make a list. Determine what you would like to improve and then hire, collaborate or find others to cover the rest. There are nine position players in baseball for a reason. Catchers don't pitch and pitchers don't play shortstop. Perhaps you're wildly creative but completely disorganized. Decide if you want to spend time getting organized (if you are even capable of this) or if the better answer is to employ someone to handle that part of the job. When you are kind to yourself, you shift away from being defensive about your weaknesses and that allows you to figure out how to compensate. No one is great at everything. Be kind and celebrate your shortcomings.

Be mindful that sometimes your greatest strength can also be your biggest weakness. The key is to know when it is working for you and when it is working against you.

Focus on the work you love to do. What gives you joy in your job? How can you do more of the work you love and less of the rest? We all have a "must do" component to our lives — the things we have to do but don't want to do (I never want to cook dinner or do the laundry but I have to!). Try to minimize these tasks and spend the smallest amount of time possible doing things you don't want to do. If you can find a way to outsource the jobs that are not your thing, do it. Be kind to yourself and walk away from the things that make you unhappy.

Don't expect everything to be 100%. Being a perfectionist is unkind. If *everything* needs to be perfect, how can you possibly achieve that?? You can't and you'll spend your days beating yourself up over small things that don't need to be perfect. Most things only need to be good enough — that's how I approach making dinner. Give your time and attention to the meaningful things and cut yourself a break on everything else.

Never compromise your values. Ever. Be kind to your moral compass and don't let anyone push you away from it. All relationships and jobs require some form of bending, but nothing should make you compromise your core values and the things that are most important to you.

No jerks allowed. Break free from bad relationships. Strive to work with good people who share your purpose, bring out the best in you and are a joy to be around. Don't accept anything less. The best part of being a leader is you get to determine who is on the team. Be kind to yourself and your team in your choices. Don't settle for jerks or duds.

This includes choosing who you work for. Let's start with the fact that some people are complete and total jerks and can't be helped. If you're reading this book, it's a good assumption you're not that type of person. You may, however, have worked for one, or you may be working for one right now. Run away fast. An abusive boss is not worth your time.

If you are in doubt, remember this quick math. If you start your career when you're 25 and work until you're 65 and change bosses every few years, you'll have 10 to 15 bosses. If you only have a shot at 15 people to learn from and be coached by, don't settle for bad bosses. It's not worth it.

Celebrate your wins. A key to outstanding leadership is celebrating success in others. Don't forget about your own. At the end of every week (or day), write down your wins — personally and professionally. Give yourself a high-five. Practice the art of celebration before you move on to the next thing.

No guilt. Try to live your life without regret. We are all imperfect. We make mistakes. We do things we wish we wouldn't have. We hurt people's feelings. We don't call our parents enough. We yell at our kids. We lose our cool. We judge. We envy others. And on and on.

Own your mistakes, settle them appropriately and move

on. Guilt and regret are dangerous and keep you rooted in the past versus the present. In order to succeed, you must be centered in today.

Have fun and find joy. The kindest thing you can do for yourself is enjoy your life. We have a limited and unknown amount of time to live — be kind and don't waste it.

Pro-Tip: Crises happen often and when they do, it can feel as if the weight of the world is on your shoulders. One of the hardest moments in my career was when the COVID-19 pandemic hit the business I was running. It took personal coaching to remind me that the collapse in the market was not my fault. It's important to take accountability and ownership of problems as a leader and it's equally as important to cut yourself a break when something strikes that is entirely out of your control. "It's not my fault" became a mantra that helped take the weight off my shoulders and allowed me to spend time and energy on what was in my control. It allowed me to move forward and focus on the problems we could solve.

THOUGHT #2: BE KIND TO YOUR STRENGTHS

Trying to get better at things you are lousy at is a waste of time. It's why I dropped math and science in Grade 10. I'm sure my parents thought it was shortsighted. But today I realize that was actually a pretty smart decision for a 14-year-old to make.

Strategy is about choice and requires saying no more than yes.

Leadership development is the same.

No business or person can excel at everything. The more you try to be all things to all people, the more watered down your purpose, values and impact become.

In coaching and development, the process somehow becomes about "fixing ourselves," which leads us to focus on shortcomings and ignore our strengths. We make a long list of the things we don't do well, develop an action plan and get to work.

Well, you know what? We have the process backwards. Instead of doubling down on improving your weaknesses, flip the exercise and put your time, attention and focus on improving your strengths from good to great.

To do: With some self-reflection and input from others, identify your strengths and weaknesses, evaluate how important each is to your success and what your growth potential is. Start with strengths first. That's the kind thing to do.

Here are some questions to get you going:

- In the past, when you made a positive impact on someone or something, what did you do?
- When you are happiest at work, what are you doing?
- How do you like to solve problems?
- If you polled your team (and go ahead and do this), what would they say about you?
- Modesty aside — what are your superpowers?
- What are your top three accomplishments and how did you make them happen?

Now think about your weaknesses and do the same exercise:

- In the past, when you made a negative impact on someone or something, what did you do?
- When you are miserable at work, what are you doing?
- Think about a time you tried to solve a problem and it backfired. What happened?
- If you polled your team (and go ahead and do this) what would they say are your weaknesses?
- What are your blind spots?
- What are your top three mistakes? What happened and what did you learn?

After you've spent some time reflecting, put together a list of your strengths and weaknesses.

The goal of the exercise is to see which skills are the most important to your success, how you rank today and where you think you can go with some focus and effort. You want to have a clear view of where you should put your development time and energy.

With some extra effort up front, you'll be able to focus on the most critical skills that will make a big impact on you, your team and your organization.

Be kind to your strengths — feed, develop and play them. They are what make you special.

> **Pro-Tip:** Your greatest strength is sometimes also your biggest weakness. For me, it's speed. For most of my career my bosses told me to slow down on decisions. I made every decision as quickly as possible and often only on gut instinct.

"Don't let the facts get in the way of a good idea" was my mantra. The upside — if you need something done quickly, I'm your person. My favourite expression? "Let's do it!" The downside — not all decisions can be made quickly and I often found myself in situations where I had to clean up the mess I made after moving too fast or, even worse, I sent others down the wrong path. Over the years, I have worked hard to become more deliberate in decision making and patient with teammates who need extra time to process information while not letting go of the need for speed, especially in today's fast-paced changing environment. Bottom line, don't be discouraged if your greatest attribute sets you off course sometimes — just be self-aware enough to think about how and when to use it.

THOUGHT #3: BE HUMAN

Sometimes the kindest thing you can do for someone is show them your flaws. This is especially true when leaders with power, privilege and rank put their hand up and ask for help, admit their weaknesses and share personal struggles with mental health. When the person in charge shows they are human, the rest of the team can breathe a sigh of relief.

The notion that leaders need to be strong, unflappable, all sunshine-and-roses and all-knowing 24/7 is flawed, unrealistic and dangerous. If the leader must be perfect and always in control, so must the rest of the team. That leads to a phony "I'm fine when I'm not" broken culture.

This doesn't mean you have to walk around bearing your

soul every minute of the day — it just means you have to be real and human.

If you don't have an answer, try "I'm not sure...what do you think?" or "I don't know...let me think about it and come back to you." Just because you're in charge doesn't mean you know everything. In fact, your job as a leader is to be curious and create enough space where others can bring forward their views and solutions. Starting with uncertainty is a powerful statement. I recently asked a teacher friend of mine how often her students throw her curveball questions. "All the time...I tell them I don't know, and we search up the answer together." Now that's leadership!

Say "I'm sorry" when you're wrong and when you've managed someone poorly. It happens, so just own it. People understand mistakes happen and they'll respect you for caring enough to apologize. Whatever you do, don't fake it or half apologize. If you were a numbskull, just say so. If you managed a situation badly, call it out. Not only are you doing the right thing but if you highlight your own flubs, why you were wrong and what you could have done better, you're building trust, leading and coaching by example throughout the process.

Acknowledge the importance of mental health and if you are open to it, share your own challenges and struggles. Half of adults experience mental illness, so the odds are whatever you are experiencing, someone else is too. Talking about issues helps eliminate the negative stigma associated and makes it easier and more comfortable for others to share their stories. Remember your job as a leader is to make the world easier for those around you.

Celebrate leaving work for a personal commitment. If

you want your team to know it's OK to cut out for a dentist appointment, to watch their kid in a school play, volunteer in the community or help an ailing parent, lead by example. Talk helps but when people see the boss leave work midday for a personal reason, they know it is OK to do the same. If you are worried people will take advantage of your flexibility — don't. The more flex you give, the more you get back in return. In my experience, people who cut out an hour early usually pay it back. It's just how human nature works. They are so grateful for the understanding, they'll do overtime to make up for it.

If you're having a lousy day don't be afraid to say so. Give yourself permission to have an off day. Just don't let mood-iness run rampant. If every day is a bad day, I'd question if you're in the right job. Leadership is hard, but the days should be mostly good. And no one wants to work for someone whose moods are unpredictable.

These are just a few starting points. The key is to remember leadership includes being human. By being vulnerable some-times and admitting you don't have it all figured out, you give permission for everyone else to do the same. Your actions will give everyone in your organization the confidence to put their hand up when they need help.

Showing you are human is one way to lead with kindness.

Pro-Tip: When I came back from parental leave after my first son was born, I asked my boss (who I adored) if I could leave work every day at 4:30. My job wasn't exactly a 9 to 5 gig, which was fine by me but I didn't want to miss dinner and bath time. My solution was to be with my son from 5pm to 7pm and then get back online to finish up what I needed to after he went to bed. My boss agreed and gave me a great piece of advice — "No problem, but make sure you tell everyone what you're doing so they understand." I sent out a note to the staff to explain my new schedule, my boundaries and how to reach me. The openness and clarity were helpful for everyone, as they were used to me being around, in the office, well past 5 pm most days. It also had a positive side effect that I didn't anticipate — it gave every other staffer permission to prioritize their personal life. "Hey, if the boss thinks dinner with family is important, maybe it's OK for me too." I became much more focused during my time in the office and with such a clear schedule, I didn't feel torn between work and home.

CHAPTER 2:

KINDNESS + HIRING

THOUGHT #4: START WITH DIVERSITY

In May 2020 George Floyd, a Black man, was murdered by a White police officer in broad daylight. It was caught on camera and it took close to a year for the murderer to be convicted. On the day of the verdict, we held our collective breath wondering whether the very clear video of a man kneeling on another man's neck for close to 10 minutes was enough evidence to prove guilt.

We live in a sometimes cruel and deeply unkind world where colour, gender, sexual orientation, religion, culture, background and income can pre-determine fate and subject some to violence, discrimination, reduced opportunities — and in some cases, murder. We often think this isn't true in democratic, highly developed countries like Canada, but it is.

Sadly, evil is everywhere.

Kindness is too. The trouble is that evil can be more contagious than kindness. Have you ever noticed how simple it is to turn a conversation negative and influence a room? Truthfully, it's easier to be negative than it is to be positive.

For many people, it's easier to be biased than it is to be open. It is easier to be racist or accept racism than it is to speak out and be anti-racist. It is easier to let a sexist or homophobic joke or slander slide versus calling it out.

Discrimination and bias exist everywhere and leaders must be aggressive, action-oriented and committed to building a diverse, inclusive culture. Best intentions are not good enough. Talk is cheap. You must show what you stand for.

Creating change within your organization is hard, and you will need some systems to get things done in a meaningful way. You can lean on your kindness superpower to help you create a safe and empathetic environment, but you're also going to need to take deliberate action. Here is a starter list of ideas that I've seen work:

Change your hiring practices. Ensure job applications are not biased to only those with experience and education. Many people can't afford to attend a top-tier university or college. That shouldn't matter. Commit to having a diverse panel of interviewers. If everyone doing the interview is the same — guess what? You're going to hire more of the same. People are inherently biased and more comfortable around others they can relate to and see themselves in.

All opinions matter. Everyone gets a voice at the table, not just the loudest, most experienced or privileged ones. Seek out diverse opinions. Go out of your way to make everyone feel comfortable, especially those who are quiet and introverted. Get comfortable with uncomfortable conversations about race, gender equity, pay gaps and discrimination. It's happening around you — don't close your eyes to it.

Recognize, call out and use your privilege. You didn't

choose to be born a man or have white privilege, but you have it, so use it. You're missing the point if you think the job of fixing the gender pay equity gap or solving racism, discrimination or bullying at work is someone else's problem. It's not. It's on those with power and privilege to fix these problems by listening to our communities, learning, showing kindness and taking action.

Be vulnerable and curious. Ask, listen and learn about other communities and cultures and don't be afraid to ask for help and guidance. Remember it's up to you to become educated.

Micromanage. Yes, that's right. Diversity is hard work and it requires your day-to-day commitment. Who does the interviewing, who makes the shortlist and who gets hired is your responsibility. It's up to you to stay on top of the details and help your team through it.

Training & Sponsorship. Set up programs targeted to enable your diverse talent to ensure they are ready to be promoted.

Feedback. Develop some type of council or feedback group that can focus on inclusion & diversity and ensure that it is getting the right amount of attention within the organization.

Having a diverse team isn't a "nice to have." Morals, justice and fairness aside, diversity is good for business. Research has proven that diversity improves revenue, productivity, creativity, innovation and more.

Remember, it is on you to own this and get it right. Use kindness to help make it happen.

Pro-Tip: Here are half a dozen of the most important things I have learned:

1. Being a good person isn't enough. Yes, of course you should be a good person, however you must stand up against bias and be deliberate in creating change in your team, organization and community.

2. We must be anti-racist, acknowledge racism exists and tear down the systems that support white supremacy. Saying "I'm not a racist" isn't enough. You must take a stand and be vocal and create change.

3. You are probably not as educated as you think. I'm embarrassed by how little I know about racism in Canada. It's on me to get educated, not on others to educate me. One of the best things I did was go out and buy a selection of books to educate myself on how to be anti-racist.

4. It's exhausting for our colleagues to share their truth to help fix a problem they didn't create and which makes them victims. We owe them thanks and gratitude for taking the time to help us. Acknowledge and appreciate their effort.

5. If you see or hear something that is offensive, say something. Laughing nervously at a racist, sexist or homophobic joke makes you an equal offender, not an innocent bystander. It's uncomfortable to do this, but it is a must-do. Sometimes the people making the comment don't even realize what they said is inappropriate — there are many common terms in the English language that were born out of racism. And don't worry if you don't take action on the spot — you can always place a

> call afterwards. The important thing is to not let it slide.
> 6. You don't get to call yourself an ally. It's not up to you to determine whether you are an ally to a community, it's up to the members to designate you an ally. Be humble in the work you do.

THOUGHT #5: TRY THE SERVER KINDNESS TEST

The most important job of a leader is to build an all-star team. Your people are the difference between success and failure, having a great culture versus a poor one, a beautiful product versus a bland user experience and good versus exceptional customer service. If you want your customers to love you, you must have a team that loves them.

Here are a few checkpoints to help you in your recruiting process:

Skillset: The obvious starting point is to ensure the candidate's skillset, experience, track record and education are a fit. Keep in mind, education shouldn't be a must-have if it isn't necessary.

Assignment: Beyond their resume, dig into their work. Find an opportunity to have the applicants perform an assignment related to the job or the business. It will give you a quick and practical understanding of their ability and a glimpse into how they think about your business. It will also demonstrate their work ethic and showcase how much care and effort they put forward.

The whole person: In addition to having the right skillset, who they are as a person is equally important. Checking references and evaluating social media profiles will help you see beyond their resume to determine if they are someone who can better your organization.

The interview process: This will give you a feel for their personality, values, how they carry themselves, their sense of humour (or lack of one), passion, listening skills, curiosity, ego, place on the team and further explore their personal background.

These are all critical steps to help determine who will do a great job for your business and be a tremendous addition to your culture.

Before you make the decision, there is one more checkpoint I call the "server kindness test."

Determining someone's character and kindness based on how they treat you, the boss, is useless. It's pretty easy to be nice to the person who will sign your paycheque. The best test is to find out how your potential employee treats the server at the restaurant during the interview. Or the receptionist and security guard at your building, the flight attendant, the UBER driver, the barista, or any critical frontline service worker.

Take the candidate out for a meal or a coffee and pay close attention to how they treat the staff. Do they look them in the eye? Do they treat them with respect? Are they curt or friendly? Do they say thank you?

Ask the receptionist or security guard what they were like when they arrived at the building.

If your recruit shows any signs of bad behaviour in these situations, this is a major red flag. Everyone has a bad day, but kind people are not the type to be rude to the server at the restaurant, for no reason.

Your role as a leader is to ensure kindness and respect

permeates its way through your entire organization. It starts with you, but you won't have the most significant impact — your team will determine the culture, so you must get hiring right.

> **Pro-Tip:** I always have my executive assistant set up my interviews, meet candidates at the door and escort them to the meeting room. If it's someone I'm thinking about hiring, I always pick their brain on what they thought of them and how they treated everyone as they walked through the building.

THOUGHT #6: WHAT HAPPENS WHEN YOU HIRE THE WRONG PERSON?

While strategy is critical to your success, the most important thing you will do as a leader is build, retain and coach a high-performing team. Often the only real competitive difference you have is your employees.

Hiring well is critical, however no one hires perfectly. A common leadership mistake is holding on for too long to an underperforming player.

We stick with them for various reasons — they are smart, have moments of greatness, were a big success somewhere else. Or maybe they moved across the country for the job, have a family, have been with the company for a long time or are going through a challenging, business situation. And, let's face it, firing someone is just awful. It's the worst part of the job. I don't know anyone who wakes up excited to terminate someone's employment. Even firing a jerk isn't easy.

You must get past these excuses. While it may be difficult and life-changing to the one person you have to let go, if you don't make a change, you impact the entire team negatively. If you think you are being kind, you're not — you are being unkind to your entire organization because you're unwilling to make a tough decision.

A weak player can prevent others from hitting their goals, which can have a financial impact and cause added stress and workload to everyone else who has to compensate for the poor performance. They are also taking up a spot that you could fill with top talent and keeping them on the team signals to your employees that a below-average contribution is acceptable. "Why am I busting my butt to achieve results when so and so can't do the job?" Not to mention, the weak player knows they aren't delivering and that doesn't feel great either.

Kindness is recognizing everyone is counting on you to surround them with all-stars. So, make the tough decision. It's your job. Once you've made the tough decision, it's time to focus on how you terminate employees with kindness.

Here is a checklist of things to contemplate.

First, is there anything else that can be done to help the struggling employee? If they are strong but in the wrong role, is there another opportunity within your company?

Assuming there isn't and you need to move on, the first step is to reach out to your HR and communications partner (if you have one) and ask yourself these questions:

- Who should deliver the message to the employee?
- What is the message? It's always better to be short and

to the point, but it is also essential to be compassionate and empathetic.

- Make sure you know exactly how you are going to start and end the meeting. While you can't predict everything, the open and close can be planned and buttoned down.
- If you can't do it in person due to a remote working situation, how can you support the employee?
- What can you do to make the exit as comfortable as possible?
- How can you help the person transition gracefully out of the role with dignity?
- Can you allow them to control the messaging about their exit? Is there an opportunity for them to personally make their own announcement?
- Don't use jargon like "we wish X all the best in her future endeavours." Ban that statement from your exit memos. That's what managers say when they don't know what else to write. If you can't say anything, whatever you do, don't say that. It's cold and people see right through it.

Throughout the process, put the employee first and stay focused on a graceful and kind exit. Do whatever you can to show kindness, empathy and compassion. Finally, when all is said and done and it is time to rehire for the position, reflect on how you can improve the role and the hiring process the second time around.

Pro-Tip: When I need to have a challenging conversation with someone, I spend time thinking about what my opening line is going to be. Often, I will say something simple, such as, "This is going to be a tough conversation." This allows the person to brace for impact and it sets the tone for the meeting.

THOUGHT #7: AND...GET RID OF THE JERKS

Take a walkabout and ask people who the abusive jerk is in the company and you'll find out pretty quickly. It's always unanimous and obvious. It's one thing everyone will agree on! "Oh yes, it's x..."

If it's so obvious, why is this person still around? And what does it say about your leadership if you allow this kind of negativity to permeate throughout the organization?

Usually, it's because the offender is a high performer, so their behaviour is tolerated. They are usually #1 at something, make the company money, and it can be hard to imagine letting them go. Sometimes, the leader just doesn't see them for who they are, maybe the manager is in denial and doesn't want to deal with the headache, or maybe they just miss the warning signs. This happens a lot with new managers who haven't yet realized people "put on shows." In other cases, the jerk is a work in progress and is being "performance managed." Basically, the leader is trying to reform them, which pretty much never works, by the way. They're broken and you need to get them off the team.

They will kill your kindness mission, crush your culture, steal ideas and clients from their colleagues, abuse their peers, hurt feelings, complain about everything and never, not once, have anyone's back unless it serves their purpose.

Yes, sometimes they are star performers achieving incredible success for the organization. But keeping them on the team is at best a short-term benefit to the bottom line. Their attitude will wreak havoc on your long-term business.

Having someone like this on the team suggests you don't care about the others, performance is the only thing that matters, and any of the values you've committed to, including kindness, integrity, honesty and inclusion, are meaningless words on a page. Culture is defined by the worst behaviour you're willing to tolerate and if you keep someone like this on the team, you're signing off on having a culture full of negative jerks.

The best part about being a leader is you get to weed these folks out. If leading with kindness is your mission, there's no way you can keep them around. This includes jerks that other people manage — if you see toxic behaviour anywhere in the organization, it's on you to ensure their manager is aware of what's going on. Nothing makes people more frustrated than watching someone like this win — so get them out and let the good ones take over the business. Use it as an opportunity to promote a rising star.

Pro-Tip: It may feel downright painful to terminate a high performing employee, even when you know you need to, but it has long-term benefits that you can't see in the storm. In my experience, the person is likely creating even more havoc than you're aware of. People are generally hesitant to complain or raise concerns about a star on the team. If management makes excuses for them, everyone stays quiet. Then when the person is let go, suddenly people open up about what else was going on and you'll wish you acted sooner.

CHAPTER 3:

KINDNESS + PEOPLE MANAGEMENT

THOUGHT #8: SETTING GOALS
YES, YOU CAN BE BOTH KIND & TOUGH

The best leaders have high expectations for themselves and their team. They push everyone to grow and achieve their goals. They have high standards and never waiver from their values. They inspire, motivate and coach top talent to exceptional performance and to be the very best possible version of themselves. Talented people are attracted to leaders who will drive them hard and make them better.

There's a way to be both a hard driver and a kind leader.

I love the spirit of this mantra, which I learned at my company — "Be kind to the people and tough on performance and issues." When you separate people from their performance, it allows you to be both kind (to the person) and tough (on expectations).

It's also a great practice to have the individual co-create what success looks like for the organization and themselves. By allowing your team to set their own performance goals (with your coaching to ensure they are focused on the right things for the business), you immediately give them control of their destiny. Top talent will set the bar high.

Your role is to ensure everyone knows what the organization is trying to achieve and help them understand how they fit into the plans. Work together to dream big and set a high bar that is both realistic and ambitious. Be generous with your time during this process and make it clear you are there in service of the employee, not the other way around.

Goals should be:

- Clear
- Achievable
- Ambitious
- Measurable
- Reviewed often
- Updated as needed

Build a reporting process that measures progress frequently. Celebrate achievements along the way and have hard, yet kind conversations when things aren't going well. Listen to input and provide constant and consistent feedback to ensure you are both clear on how things are going.

Now that the performance goals are set, it's time to get good at giving feedback.

Pro-Tip: Goals are tricky. It's easy to write down "be #1" or "win the World Series" and it's easy to measure both — you either win the WS or you don't, you are either in first place or you aren't. However, you need to be mindful that while these *are* goals, you need a way to measure the inputs that will help you achieve these goals. What will it take for you to win the World Series? Trade for a reliever? Improve the training facilities? Lead the league in home runs? And how can you measure those inputs along the way? Goals can be empty without a path to achievement for each person. We've all been on teams that go through a bout of losing where you can't seem to get positive momentum going. When this happens, consider changing up your goals. Sometimes the big goal is daunting or maybe it's uninspiring — I've been part of plans where the goals we had were too cold-hearted because they were just a bunch of numbers on a page. One trick is to try setting smaller, achievable actions that can be measured and celebrated. This can allow you to start getting some wins under your belt and help the team get their confidence back.

THOUGHT #9: KINDNESS IN FEEDBACK

One of my colleagues is famous for saying, "feedback is a gift." We sometimes use the phrase as code to make us laugh when one of us is about to get schooled on something we did that wasn't exactly a home run. "Remember Julie...feedback is a gift!"

Feedback *is* a gift.

Constructive, meaningful feedback is *the* kindest thing you can do for a teammate.

Every person needs objective input on their work, ideas

and how they show up in front of others. We all have blind spots in how we present ourselves and the way we view our work. We get comfortable and lose objectivity. Ever proofread something 10 times, only for someone else to read it once and find a typo you didn't spot? That's why feedback is so important. Not to catch your mistakes but to help you see yourself differently and challenge you to think about something from a different angle. Sometimes we can't see ourselves as clearly as others can.

Think about the team professional athletes have working for them — coaches, managers, trainers, doctors, therapists, agents, financial advisors, media coaches — all focused on helping the player get a competitive edge. As the head coach, your team needs you to provide meaningful feedback to help them achieve their goals and perform higher.

But not all feedback is helpful and most of us give terrible advice from time to time.

Ask a lot of questions. Before you wind up and let the feedback fly, ask what the intention was. "What were you trying to achieve?" "How did you feel about the work?" "What would you do differently if you started again?" "Why did you take this approach?" More often than not people know what worked and what didn't and asking many questions will allow them to come to their conclusions. This coaching approach puts the power and control back into the person's hands and will enable them to improve their work on their own. This approach also allows you to stay away from solving other people's problems. Even the best leaders don't always give great advice and no one person has the solution to everything. Your job is to guide and coach. It's the team's job to solve problems.

Don't be too positive. If you think you're kind by only giving praise, you're wrong. Do you think Vladimir Guerrero Jr.'s hitting coach tells him every swing is perfect? There's a reason why ballplayers attend batting practice. Top talent needs constructive input to help them get better. Only telling them how great they are isn't going to help anyone. Plus, they don't believe it.

Be specific, not generic. "That was great" and "That was bad" doesn't help anyone. Be clear with your commentary. Call out precisely what went well and why. Why was it great? What made it ineffective?

Be selective. It may be tempting to throw a whole bunch of things to fix at someone, but this isn't effective. There is only so much one person can take in at a time. Be realistic in how many things someone can work on, be empathetic and don't overwhelm them with a long list of things to fix. Pick one or two most important areas.

Be consistent. This is a no-brainer; however, we're all guilty of being inconsistent with feedback.

Don't tell someone one thing one day and the exact opposite the next unless you have a good reason for the change. There are times when you need to change course and if that's the case, be sure to call it out. "I know I said this... however after x happened, I think you should consider..."

Watch your moods. We all have good days and bad days. Your mood can drastically change your view on something. Body language, emotion and tone all play a significant factor when giving input. Be conscious of how you feel before you start a coaching session. If you're in a terrible mood, perhaps reschedule.

Be kind with your words. No matter what, ask your questions and deliver your input with kindness. Remember kind doesn't mean positive — it simply means you will be present throughout the discussion and think deeply about how your words will impact the other person. Don't shy away from the tough stuff — the kindest thing you can do for someone is give consistent, specific, balanced feedback explicitly designed to help your all-star be their very best. Kindness will allow you to focus on the other person and do whatever is best for them.

If you can't be kind, be quiet. If you can't deliver a message or feedback with kindness, especially in a group setting, stay silent until you figure out how you can. Short of someone committing something entirely and utterly offside that needs a different approach, find a way to stay true to your kindness north star. Even if it means saying, "I'm not sure how I feel about this, let me think about it and get back to you." We think we need an answer for everything, all the time, on the spot. Well, we don't and overreacting to something in the moment will cause more harm than it's worth. According to research, for every negative interaction you have with someone, you need FIVE positive ones, so think before you speak.

If you're unsure if what you're about to say is kind enough, the odds are it isn't, so take a pause. When in doubt, imagine your words are going to end up on social media. If it concerns you, rethink your approach. Take your time — it's worth it.

> **Pro-Tip:** If you're unsure how to offer feedback to someone, here's a quick trick — just ask. "Are you open to some

feedback?" I've never met a person who hasn't said yes
to this. That question gives you an easy way to open the
dialogue.

THOUGHT #10: KINDNESS IN FEEDBACK — THIS TIME FOR THE BOSS

It's OK to be nice to your boss. Seriously. I know it's often
considered "sucking up" if you are friendly and complimentary
to the person in charge, but I don't buy it. I think it's old-fash-
ioned and dangerous to build a mentality where employees
feel management is against them, so they don't get too close.

Instead, you should treat your boss with kindness and
empathy. A business title doesn't replace the need for feedback,
positive reinforcement and camaraderie from colleagues at
work. Leaders and founders carry a lot of weight on their shoulders and usually have the smallest support system to lean on
within the organization. "It's lonely at the top" is a real thing.

You have spent a lot of time practicing how to lead your
team with kindness.

To truly commit, you must extend it to everyone.

By "everyone" I mean your team, your customers *and* your
boss. So, get on with it!

Here are a few simple ways to get you started:

Always be genuine. Don't change your personality when
talking to your boss. You shouldn't show up as a completely
different person when the audience changes. Of course we
all adjust some things, in certain company — how you talk
in front of your grandmother may differ from the words you

use with friends, but in both cases you don't fundamentally change who you are. This holds true at work. Whether it's your team or your boss, you must be you.

Offer positive feedback. Just because it was the boss's idea, doesn't mean it doesn't need validation. Share your praise on ideas that are working well within the organization and pass along constructive input on how to improve other areas.

Lend a hand. When it's obvious the organization is going through a tough patch, step up and ask the leader how they are doing and if you can help.

Celebrate. Don't be afraid to celebrate a big win with a congrats note to your boss.

There is no mystery to this, it's as simple as showing the same kindness you show to your team, but to your boss. If you lead with kindness, no one will mistake it for "sucking up" and if they do, that's their problem.

Pro-Tip: Stop overthinking your relationship with your boss. You shouldn't have to think long and hard about how a compliment or a comment comes across. Or how you will position an issue. Talking to your boss should be easy, natural and helpful. If it isn't, it is probably worth evaluating. Is it you or is it them? Of course, it takes time to be fully at ease around anyone, but your relationship with your boss shouldn't be all that different from others. You should be able to be yourself regardless of the hierarchy of a relationship and if your boss doesn't accept that, I'd suggest you find a

new one. By the way, everyone can figure out quickly who
is genuine and who is full of it.

THOUGHT #11: JUDGEMENT IS NOT KIND

Judgement is the kryptonite to kindness. It's a kindness killer.

What is judgement?

Judgement is NOT an informed point of view.

Judgement is NOT an informed opinion.

Judgement is NOT constructive feedback.

Judgement does NOT inspire innovation or new ideas.

Judgement is gossip. "Did you see/read /hear what so &
so did?"

Judgement is biased. "He ALWAYS does x, y and z."

Judgement is rooted in fear of new and novel ideas. "That
will never work" was said about airplanes, mobile phones,
personal computers, the Beatles, online shopping, overnight
package delivery and more.

Judgement is unkind.

The fastest way to lose the credibility and trust you have as
a leader is to consistently place judgement on your team's work,
ideas, feelings and the people themselves, without seeking to
understand information or context. Leaders low on curiosity and high on judgement will demotivate their team, crush
innovation and idea generation. No one wants to be judged
unfairly, especially when it is done without understanding
their process and perspective.

In addition to killing culture, if you're placing judgement
without being curious, you are coming to false conclusions

and missing opportunities that are damaging your business.

Every organization needs new ideas and innovation. It's your job to help turbocharge your team and enable them to test, try and learn.

Be kind to new ideas and don't place judgement; instead, act like a two-year-old.

Ask why, then ask it again and again and again. Help your team answer the why behind the idea.

Ultimately you need to care more about how your judgement makes the other person feel and less about how it makes you feel. A leader's role isn't to be judge and jury or the smartest person in the room — it's to bring out the best in those around you.

Pro-Tip: What others say about others behind their back, they also say about you, behind yours. It is a telltale sign; when someone is gossiping or judging another person with you, they are doing the same about you to someone else. Don't fall for it. It's a major red flag and a sign you can't trust them. Be cautious around people who bad-mouth their former employers or colleagues, especially if they do it during an interview. Be astute enough to understand whatever they say about others, they will say about you too, one day.

THOUGHT #12: BE KIND AND SAY NO

Many leaders find it challenging to say no to their team, especially if you are a people pleaser like me. It can feel counterintuitive to say no when striving to enable innovation, new ideas, accountability and autonomy within your team. You want people to make their own decisions and hold them accountable versus micromanaging their moves. You also want them to learn from their mistakes. Pushing accountability and decision-making throughout the organization is the right thing to do and a sign of outstanding leadership — however, there are times when you need to say no.

When you are sure a decision is wrong or off base and will negatively impact the organization, you may need to step in and say no. While it may feel uncomfortable, use your kindness lens to help you.

Think about how the person on your team will feel if their decision, which you know is wrong, hurts their teammates by costing the company financially and resulting in layoffs. Or the mistake forces others to step in and work overtime to resolve the problem. Or maybe the initiative is simply a distraction and not in line with your plans or strategy, making the organization spin and spend time on something that isn't a priority.

Remember you are in the role for a reason — to use your smarts and experience to lead others to success. Sometimes saying no is the best way to do this. When it is, it is your responsibility to step in. The trick is to make the situation a learning experience for your employee.

Spend as much time as necessary to coach your employee through the decision. Remember, kindness in leadership means you're not going to bark orders at people, instead you're going to put in the work to help the person come to the right solution. Challenge them through curiosity. Ask them to play out the decision to the end. Ask them to think about what success will look like and to think through what could go wrong. Continue to work with them until they are clear on the risk and the impact it could have on their teammates. With the right amount of scenario planning, your employee will get to a good place without you having to say no and they'll be proud of themselves for the save.

Of course, there are times when you can't always get someone to the decision you're looking for and you may need to make the call, in service to the business or the bigger group. If that's the case, be kind and firm on your decision. Explain your rationale and reasons and move on.

While your goal as a leader should be to say yes, not no, there are times when you must make a judgement call and it's OK. It's your job.

> **Pro-Tip:** If you have a hard time saying no, like me, and find yourself agreeing to things you shouldn't, get good at saying, "let me think about it" or "is it OK if I think about things for a day or two?" This will buy you some time to dig into what you want to do instead of making a fast — usually yes — decision that you regret or must retract.

THOUGHT #13: KINDNESS AND FAILURE

Let's be honest — it sucks to fail.

When your performance is measured often and openly, it can be so painful!

For most of us, failure hurts our confidence and creates fear in trying new ideas and in some cases, it can cost you your job.

With stakes that high, who would possibly want to try something new if there's even a remote chance you will fail? What is the upside?

It's curious despite these pitfalls and stigmas that when you Google search "failure is" this is what shows up:

Failure is the key to success...

Failure is the stepping stone to success...

Failure is the mother to success...

Failure is not fatal...

How can failure be necessary for success yet have such awful outcomes and emotions attached to it?

When we dig deep, it isn't usually failing that is painful, it is the fallout that hurts.

Unfortunately, blame happens often because the human instinct is to blame someone or something when things go wrong. Leaders often do it to prove they have the situation in hand. "Don't worry...heads will roll over this..." When things aren't going well in business, blame is the one thing a leader has control over.

But do great leaders discipline their team when they step out on a new idea or innovation and fail? Do the best leaders devalue someone's self-worth simply because they tried a unique approach? Do leaders believe all-star talent will be inspired and motivated by the shame and blame game?

Not a chance.

Instead, the best leaders remove the negative backlash from failure and replace it with kindness and celebration.

Even in life-and-death situations, there is an opportunity to do this. While we may never celebrate the outcome of losing a patient on the operating table, a medical team can applaud and recognize the tireless effort and show kindness to those who gave it everything they had. When the time is right, the team can also step away and objectively identify what went wrong, why it happened and learn from the mistake to prevent it from happening again. Great teams will also make their failures known to deter others from the same error.

In non-life-and-death situations, we should go one step further and acknowledge those who fail when trying out new ideas. Leaders should push their team to test and try, fail fast, iterate and try again. Winning teams should have the security and support to create and test new solutions for their customers and when they don't work out, not stress over what the boss will think.

Because the boss will be kind enough to say, "Nice try...what did you learn and where are you going next? I'm with you."

When you're kind in failure, your team will happily keep swinging and eventually knock it out of the park. If you're not, you'll end up stuck and terrified to step out.

FAIL FAST. BE KIND. FAIL AGAIN.

Pro-Tip: I botched a decision that cost our company a ton of money when I fired a popular morning host who had been with the radio station for decades. My goal was to refresh the sound and try something new and it was a total disaster. (Google it!)

I'm sure the only reason I didn't get fired was that no one could figure out how to fix the problem! I got the "You f*#^ed it, you fix it" speech. For a period of time it was all anyone would talk to me about. I (this isn't a joke) went into labour at the office and when I got home to get my things, our cleaner was there. She looked me dead in the eye and said, "I've been reading about you in the news and it isn't good." I then went on to talk her through the decision between contractions. When I arrived at the hospital, the nurse asked me what I did for a living and I said I didn't want to talk about it. I was in too much pain to have to explain my decision yet again. After a brutal couple of years, I managed to hire the host back and make things right.

If I had the chance, I'd do it all over again (minus explaining my strategy while in labour). That colossal failure taught me more in 12 months than I learned in decades.

Here's what I learned.

1. **Own it.** I didn't make the decision in isolation, but it was my mistake. I accepted it. I didn't deflect blame or make a bunch of excuses or bad-mouth anyone. I also never once tried to create a story that justified my decisions.

2. **Nice try**. As much as the decision was the wrong one, it was a great try. I took a swing at a big move, changing up a heritage radio station morning show, infusing some fresh thinking and it didn't work. Outside of its impact on the people — which I don't feel great about — it was a good try.

3. **There's always a way out of the ditch.** Someone once told me the measure of a person is not how they ended up in the ditch, but how they get out. Swing, miss, try again, home run!

4. **Execution is as important as strategy**. I'm not sure the

strategy was completely wrong, but I know for sure the execution was downright awful, right down to how I let the host know we were cancelling the show.

5. **Don't let your ego get the best of you.** The only thing I did right in all of this was I didn't let pride or ego get in the way of making things right. Two things became apparent to me: 1) I owed the host an apology and an explanation for why I made the decision; 2) Bringing her back was a great idea. Many people think apologizing or admitting failure will end their careers or be embarrassing. This isn't true. Failing to admit when you're wrong is much more likely to lead to missed opportunities.

6. **When in doubt, just tell the truth.** When the time came to draft the email to the public to share the news, I needed a "story" to explain what happened. After staring at my keyboard for a very long time, with an impending deadline and no good ideas, I decided to try out the truth. I opened with "Have you ever made a mistake at work?" Being a terrible liar, I had no idea how to turn an undeniable mistake into some kind of marketing story, so I wrote from the heart. It wasn't a calculated decision, but it turned out to be a pivotal moment in my leadership journey. When in doubt, just be you and don't be afraid to write and speak from the heart.

The story has a happy ending. The host's return brought us straight back to #1, I made the company its money back and some extra dollars for good measure and we went on to have a fantastic relationship, which continues to this day.

CHAPTER 4:

KINDNESS + TEAM

THOUGHT #14: KINDNESS AS A VALUE

It is vital to define a set of values for your team, the core beliefs in which you will operate your business and build your culture. Having clearly defined values will help you determine if your company and team are on the right path and the values you set will determine the direction of your company and team.

Defining your company and team values is critical work that requires considerable time, energy and thinking. Your values don't change every six months — this isn't an action plan you reset every year. Start with kindness as a value (of course!) and immediately use it with your team. Instead of doing this work on your own, show your team kindness by involving them in the process and giving them a seat at the table. They will appreciate having input into how the company and culture is shaped, and it will also improve the process as you'll have diverse input on how best to serve your customers and build your culture.

Once you define your values, never, ever, ever let anyone push you off of them. This is an area where compromise can't happen. When you hold firm on your values, you will ensure that you spend your time, energy and resources on the things and people who mean the most to you. Having clearly defined values also makes decision making easier. You and your team will sleep well by making values-based decisions.

Pro-Tip: Ideally, you want your personal values to line up with your company and team values to ensure you won't be conflicted in your personal and professional life. Here are mine to help you get started:

1. Kindness
2. Creativity
3. Honesty (my Mom told me at a young age I was a terrible liar and should give it up.)
4. Positivity/Optimism
5. Fun/Humour
6. Curiosity
7. Fairness
8. Competition

THOUGHT #15: USE KINDNESS TO BUILD TRUST & ALWAYS TELL THE TRUTH

Tell me what I need to hear, not what I want to hear.

The only way to build an all-star team and successful business is to have a culture where people tell the truth. No matter how hard or painful. So often, people will shy away from tough, uncomfortable conversations because they are hard. Shying away from these discussions ultimately leads to poor decisions, missed opportunities, cover-up, bad behaviour and superficial, dysfunctional relationships. If the truth is only whispered and anonymous or said behind closed doors, or the group isn't comfortable speaking up in a meeting and wait until afterwards, in smaller circles, to speak their minds, you have a problem. This behaviour leads to decisions getting overturned without everyone knowing what's going on.

Use kindness to help you surface the truth throughout the organization.

Kindness will help you build trust more quickly. When people see you as someone who always treats them with kindness and cares deeply about their success and the business's success, it makes it easier for them to trust you. Your agenda is clear — you are in service of the team and the company. Once you establish trust, it will be easier for people to speak their minds, challenge and debate assumptions and ideas, bring forward new thinking and innovation, stand up for others and call out bad behaviour. Trust gives everyone the confidence to speak the truth and know there will not be any repercussions. This openness will ensure the best decisions are made for the company and the people.

Kindness will also help make the tough conversations a little easier. People dodge confrontation because it's uncomfortable. Not everyone wants to be on the debate team. Most are happiest when things are going smoothly and everyone agrees. Few people enjoy pushing the boundaries and challenging the status quo. When you find these disruptors in your organization, wrap your arms around them, give them development opportunities, stretch assignments and most importantly, a chance to speak their truth. It takes courage to push back, especially against authority. Those who challenge the status quo will keep you honest at every turn. Show them kindness and make their voice heard. Show equal kindness to those struggling to speak their minds. They are valuable to the company and need a mechanism to open up. Help them get comfortable with debate. Give them a voice at the table. If they are always quiet in a meeting, ask them questions to help bring out their viewpoint. Celebrate and thank them when they share their thoughts, especially in public.

When you can get everyone pushing each other and debating core decisions, that's where the magic happens in an organization.

When everyone speaks the truth, you cut out the BS, get to the heart of the issues which plague your customers and your employees and speed up progress.

I don't believe in the old business mantra, "sometimes you have to lie." You can always say "I can't tell you that right now"... but you never have to lie. Ever.

Trust is the foundation for every strong relationship — without it, you can't succeed.

Pro-Tip: If you're feeling uncomfortable about speaking your mind and taking a different position from someone, either in a group or one-on-one setting, try calling out your feelings and asking a question first. Here are a few examples of how I might approach this: "Are you open to a different point of view?" "I am going out on a limb here...and I'm a bit nervous doing so, but I'd love to give you a different perspective if you're open to it." "Permission to be provocative? Share a different viewpoint? Challenge that idea?" Asking a question can also help make things more comfortable for others. I like to speak my mind and challenge thinking, but I never want to make anyone feel badly, feel attacked or think that their idea isn't worthwhile. I find this approach makes it easier to have debates and difficult conversations, as it delivers a cue that a differing opinion is coming next.

THOUGHT #16: BE A TIME HERO

Time is the most important currency.

It is finite and limited.

You can never get it back. Not a minute, not a second, not an hour.

Yet, we waste time and then we beg to have it back.

Just one more day, week, month, year.

"If only I would have..." We all say that at various times in our lives.

Your job as a leader is to give time the respect it deserves.

You are responsible for saving, not costing, your team time.

If you waste someone's time, you are stealing from them.

Think of it as robbery!

Here's a trick — imagine you must personally pay for your team's time. Let's call it a buck-a-minute.

Hold a one-hour meeting with five people and you're out $300. Hold a 30-minute meeting with 15 people and you're out $450.

It's not even lunch and you are already broke!

When you waste someone's time, just remember you are taking away the one thing they can *never* get more of.

Instead of being a bandit, be a hero.

Be the TIME HERO. Show your team kindness by respecting and valuing their time.

Fix your meetings. Don't call them unnecessarily and when you do have meetings, make them short, with an agenda, a purpose and desired outcome and as skinny an invite list as possible. Use the "optional" feature in online calendars and give non-essential participants the choice to determine if it's worth their time.

Don't have a meeting when a quick note will do. If you can give people the information they need in writing, you don't need to meet.

This is hard work but when we get it right, it's incredible.

Learn how to work your tech. Don't hold up a team because you can't figure out how to turn on your mic or camera or the presentation tech. If handling tech is something you just find too difficult, then make sure you arrange for tech support.

Stop repeating yourself. People are smart and heard what you said the first time! Repetition is a hard habit to break — it may be the way you form your thoughts — but when you say the same thing over and over, it's a waste of everyone else's time and it devalues your point. If you're trying to convince yourself and need to talk things through, acknowledge you're doing this and ask for permission, patience and feedback.

You will never go wrong by getting your point across faster.

Be a great listener. Listen before you speak. Don't repeat what others have already said. Here is a common mistake we all make in meetings — "I have nothing to add... except..." and then you go on and repeat what the person before you just said. Instead, a simple "totally agree with that" is way better. You have two ears and a mouth. Use them accordingly. And don't cut people off when they're speaking.

Save the non-urgent, late-night or weekend "I have a great idea" message. Stick them in drafts and send them the next business day if warranted. Often on second reading they aren't worth sending and holding them until the next business day helps keep your team from spinning, especially when they should be having some downtime.

Stop saying "do you have a minute?" It's likely you need 15 or 30.

Quit nit-picking. Get away from nagging over unimportant details and asking for meaningless changes. Most things are subjective, and your way is not likely better. Asking for endless rewrites and drafts of material should only happen when the changes are required and make a difference to the final product.

Be on time. Always. No one is perfect, but it's wrong to be late.

Now that you're a time hero, for every minute you give someone back, imagine they are paying you a dollar.

It's not even lunch and you're up a thousand bucks. Feels better, doesn't it?

Think about your own time too. It is equally important to be kind with your own time. You are not getting it back.

Ask yourself these questions:

- Where am I spending my time? Be brutally honest with yourself. Write it down and evaluate it.

- What did I accomplish?
- Was it meaningful?
- Was it fun?
- Was it what I call "busy work" — the work you do when you're not sure what else to do or when you're tired and just filling time?
- Who did I spend it with? If I could do it again, would I spend it with them?

If you're not happy with your answers most of the time, you are cheating yourself and deserve better. How would you *like* to spend your time? Figure it out and then go and do that. Whether it is your time, or someone else's, be kind and use it well.

Pro-Tip: The only way I can manage my time is by setting clear boundaries on what I will and won't do. The focus and rules have changed over the years, but the process hasn't. I believe you can enjoy a fulfilling career and a nice personal life, but you have to consciously work at it. Here are some personal examples of how I have made choices to optimize my time and make it easy for me to know when to say no and not feel guilty about it.

Kids: I am lucky — I was able to choose when to have kids. I decided to wait until I was in my 30s and spent my 20s focused on career and socializing. When my kids were born, I swapped out weekends with friends for parenting and shifted my priority to family and work. I can manage parenting and a demanding career, but I had to give up my robust social life. In the early days, I chose to socialize and have a career, but I couldn't have added kids to that mix.

Travel: I love to travel and do a fair amount of business trips; however, I only agreed to take on more work after my kids were old enough to handle me being away. We also swapped couple and friend trips for family vacations. Now I'm focused on business and family travel.

Email: I stopped subscribing to newsletters (sports, news, entertainment) using my work email, even if the subscription is for my job. This makes it easy to delineate between reading news updates on my personal account versus responding and taking action on my work account. I am also diligent about unsubscribing to email I don't want. Sure, it's easy to delete them, but even that is a waste of time.

Sports: I like to play sports. But I couldn't find time when my kids were young, so I shifted from playing to coaching their baseball teams. It allowed me to stay in the game but be with them. When they stopped playing, I started up again.

These are small tricks that work for me. It's important that you find your own life and work hacks. But make sure you do work at this — I've seen too many people sacrifice a good personal life for taking on too much work.

THOUGHT #17: GET YOUR FACE OUT OF YOUR PHONE

Why is screen time relevant to leadership and kindness?

There is no more insulting move than stuffing your face

in your screen when someone is talking. This is absolutely a show of anti-kindness.

With one move, you have signaled: your ideas don't matter, what you're saying isn't interesting, you are wasting my time, your words are unnecessary and you are not important.

Imagine you're in a boardroom having a meeting with a group, someone is making a presentation and you reach into your bag and pull out a physical book, flip it open and start reading. You turn the pages while the person at the front of the room is sharing work that took them 30 hours to prepare.

What if you were in the middle of a conversation with a colleague and you start to flip through a physical newspaper looking for the baseball box scores?

There would be no debate about who the complete jerk is.

Grabbing for a book, magazine or newspaper sounds outrageous doesn't it? But is it any more disrespectful than dropping your head into your phone while someone is speaking?

No, it isn't. To the person speaking, it's all the same and it signals their work, time and opinion isn't valued. It's soul destroying. Yet we have come to accept it's OK. We're all guilty of it. I catch myself doing it often.

The worst offense is when someone only looks up to speak in a meeting and when done talking, drops back into their screen. This screams, "I'm better than you and so important that I will only look you in the eye when I'm speaking." It's unlikely that's the intention of their action, but intent isn't always reality.

If you want to lead with kindness, break this habit. Here are a few easy ways to get started.

Lay some ground rules around screen use during

meetings and interactions. It is OK to take digital notes on your screen, it's not OK to answer emails or check social media. It's OK to search relevant material online during a meeting but not OK to shop online. If there's a reason why you think multitasking is OK, state why upfront. There are times when it may make sense, but if you don't call it out, it's disrespectful.

Showcase good behaviour. If you want people to adopt a phone-free meeting, don't use your phone in a meeting yourself!

Question/call out bad behaviour. You can usually tell when someone is engaged and using a device as an aid versus getting other work done. As a leader, ask the person after the meeting if they were distracted and why. Show them kindness and give them the benefit of the doubt; most people are not shopping, they are multi-tasking. Maybe they have too much work on their plate, or perhaps the meeting wasn't relevant. Ask if there's something you can do to help them stay focused. It's also worth talking to them about how it likely made the presenter feel looking at the top of their head.

When you find many others multitasking during a presentation or meeting, get curious and ask why. Is the invite list too broad? Are people in meetings they don't need to attend? Maybe the presentation was unnecessary and would be better sent out via email and the meeting time used for discussion. Or perhaps the meeting was unnecessary. Was the presentation or presenter boring or hard to follow or the content irrelevant? If so, offer constructive feedback. Chase down why this is happening.

We've all become so accustomed to picking up our phones, that the average user unlocks their phone 150 times a day. We let it get in the way of our relationships and even those with the most discipline, the biggest hearts and the best manners still slip.

Don't do it.

Show kindness, find a way to break the habit, and build a culture where the entire team works together to improve in this area.

Pro-Tip: Here's a trick I implemented that helped me improve my focus and stay present (I'm not perfect!). Turn off all notifications on your devices. I personally only leave text on — my kids, team and boss know this is how to reach me if there's an emergency. Everything else must wait until I'm ready to check in. I've yet to meet anyone who can ignore notifications!

THOUGHT #18: BE FLEXIBLE

Want to show kindness? Show flexibility.

In work hours.

In location.

In communication.

In praise.

In discipline.

In one-on-one meetings.

In team meetings.

In everything but your values.

People are unique — it is a mistake to have a one-size-fits-all approach to leadership and managing people.

Treat everyone fairly but don't treat them all the same.

Some people love fanfare, public recognition and praise in front of a crowd. Others prefer a quieter approach, maybe a handwritten card, some kudos in front of a few close colleagues or a quick text message.

Some like to work alone, without interruption and others want to be in the middle of the action to feed off the energy of those around them. Many like a combination of the two.

You'll have one person on your team who loves to share personal stories and pictures of their kids and pets, but then you'll have another who draws a firm line between work and home, sharing next to no personal information.

Some like to bounce half-baked ideas off anyone and everyone and others who aren't comfortable sharing and asking for feedback until they have a fully formed plan. Those happy to brainstorm on the spot on any topic, throw ideas out a dime a dozen and then there are introverted thinkers who need to go away and ponder before they offer up their opinion.

Many are evening and weekend workers — it's when they do their best thinking or have a more manageable personal schedule to get work done and others who want to shut off outside traditional office hours.

Some people give trust before it is earned, others won't give an inch until proven.

And everyone has personal commitments and hobbies they want to work around.

The list goes on and on. The bottom line? It's OK — diversity in teams makes us better, so embrace it. Your job as a leader, is to be in service of your team, which means getting to know exactly what each person needs and wants and then customize accordingly. Here are a few example areas where you can show kindness through flexibility:

Communication: Develop a deep understanding of how your team members like to communicate. Some like to write reports, others want to sit down and talk it through.

Stress: Determine what makes them anxious and what their stressors are. Recognizing stress in your teammates, especially those you manage directly, is crucial. You'll be a better support system if you learn to see the warning signs in your people.

Inspiration: Learn what gets them motivated and inspired and what gives them energy, comfort and joy.

Personal time: Understand their commute and external commitments and how you can provide some flexibility to help them better balance their work and personal life.

Kudos: Figure out how they like to be recognized and shown appreciation.

Pay attention. Don't be afraid to ask a lot of questions — people are generally open when you ask them for feedback. Embrace customization and give employees as much flexibility as possible. When you remove unnecessary boundaries and rules, people return the kindness with a more profound commitment to the team, business and company.

Pro-Tip: Outside of shift work that starts and ends at a certain time, I have never been a fan of regulating office hours. I had an employee once tell me that their former boss, at a different company, used to make them stay at the office until a certain time, for no reason, regardless of whether they had work to do or not. It led to mistrust and a waste of time. My philosophy is to evaluate the work, not the hours. It's easy to regulate hours at the office, and perhaps you feel more in control by doing this, but I prefer to measure the output of the work, not where and when people made it happen.

THOUGHT #19: THE KIND COLLABORATOR OR THE IDEA HOG?

We've all met the idea hog.

The leader who refuses to run with something unless it is their idea. They fake interest in other people's opinions but rarely help action them. They may not realize they're doing it — but everyone else sees it.

Don't be the idea hog — be the kind collaborator.

Collaboration is critical to the success of a business. As we've seen time and time again, the best ideas come from some sort of partnership. Even solo artists have a team of people behind the scenes helping them.

Whether it is Converse and Tyler the Creator, Elton John and Bernie Taupin or Tina Fey and Amy Poehler, what the two achieved together was incredible with each person bringing their own creativity, problem solving and diverse point of view.

The same is true for you and your team. By matching and meshing skillsets, you have the opportunity to take an idea from good to great. Collaboration is also vital in building trust. When you're willing to pass the credit, adopt the mantra "the best idea wins" and celebrate your teammates, you earn respect and trust from those around you.

Be the leader who is first to encourage others to offer ideas, helps build the ideas through coaching and feedback, offers resources to get them to market and celebrates success.

People will learn quickly you care more about the team than you do yourself and will happily bring their best ideas forward to serve the business and delight the customer.

Pro-Tip: Take every possible opportunity you can to give people credit for their work. Humans love coming up with ideas and getting credit for innovation. As a leader, it's a privilege to celebrate someone's work.

Seek out the owner of the original idea and show kindness through celebration.

Here are the four ways I like to credit and show off the work of others:

1. Messaging. Drop them a note via email, text or chat — either privately or copy others.
2. Social media. One of the most effective ways to praise your team is through social media. It's a terrific forum to give someone credit in public.
3. A weekly newsletter highlighting the work of others is circulated to my team.
4. And one I don't see enough — in a meeting, when someone's idea is being talked about, jump in and ensure the person gets credit with "that was x's idea." It's even more powerful if the person who came up with the idea is in the room.

I'll never fully understand why it is so hard for people

to celebrate or recognize others' ideas. Use your kindness lens and think about how you feel when someone credits your work and do the same.

THOUGHT #20: LEADING A TEAM THROUGH TURBULENCE

It is easier to lead a team during good times when business is growing, the market is healthy and you have tailwinds behind you. It's also easier to practice kindness when things are going well. The real measure of kindness comes when things are not going well and market conditions are turbulent. How do you, as a leader, behave with your team then? The COVID-19 pandemic highlighted outstanding (and awful) leadership. It was easy to pick out the executives and managers who were making smart decisions on the fly. They put the safety of their customers and team first. They led their people with kindness and empathy, as everyone tried desperately to balance work and family while juggling deadlines, cancellations and ever-changing restrictions.

Whether you are going through a pandemic or a routine crisis, your leadership is needed more than ever during difficult times. When times are turbulent, a leader must be the north star for the organization — a steady head and hand to keep the team on track and provide hope, input and resources to ride things out.

Here are a few ways you can use kindness to help manage during turmoil:

Be consistent. Your emotional control is always critical, especially during a crisis. The last thing a team needs is a moody, unpredictable leader. Remember leading with kindness means putting other people first, not yourself. Don't be the "I wonder which version of X we're going to get today" type of manager.

Over-communicate. Don't leave people flip-flopping in the wind, wondering what is going on. Even if you don't have any new information, find a way to show up with a check-in. Schedule optional all-hands meetings frequently to give updates and take questions. It's incredible what 10 minutes together, every day, will do to quash fear and keep the team calm and nimble. Giving people the option to attend is also a powerful tool.

Reach out to people across the organization just to say hi and ask how they are doing. Technology has made it easy to message anyone on staff with an informal note or video chat.

Ask these two questions every chance you get: How are you really doing? Is there one thing I can do to help you? Ask everyone, customers too. These questions are more specific than "how are you?" and "can I help?" People defer to "fine" and "no, I'm OK" when they get the generic version.

If someone is uncharacteristically making a lot of mistakes or dropping the ball, be kind and give them the benefit of the doubt. Don't judge or criticize too quickly. There's likely something else going on. Pull them aside and ask how they are doing and if you can help. You have no idea what is going on in their world. Find a way to get to the truth but remember — asking once may not get you there.

Pay attention to body language. People will often say they are OK, but exhaustion and burnout are hard to hide physically. Do they look tired? Are their arms crossed? Are they late to meetings? Do they seem frazzled or frantic in conversation? Are they low on energy?

Find a way to keep things fun and light. Not every meeting during a crisis can be a downer. People need a break and need to laugh. Keep in mind, however, that this approach is not appropriate if someone is going through a personal crisis or loss.

Don't manage everyone the same. Remember your flexibility muscle. Some people in crisis will throw themselves into work. Be respectful of their decision. It may be the one thing keeping them afloat. On the flip side, some people need more downtime to manage through a difficult time. Get to know who needs what and be prepared when people change their minds. That's the problem with a crisis — it's unpredictable.

Be kind to yourself. There are times when *you* will need to call a timeout. Don't be afraid to do it. Rest, exercise and time away will help you build the stamina you need to lead the organization. Whenever you take time off, or ask for help, you model positive behaviour for others. It's a lot easier taking a vacation when your boss is doing the same. Often during a crisis, people believe that working harder or working more is the right thing to do — there comes the point where putting in more hours actually hurts the organization more than it helps.

Be realistic. Sometimes people need to hear, "don't worry everything will be OK," but when you know it won't, you need to tell people the truth and provide a plan of action.

Pro-Tip: I could write an entire book about what I learned managing through COVID-19. It has been the biggest crisis I've experienced in my career. Here are a few of the key lessons I learned that can be used in any crisis, not just a pandemic:

Uncertainty is brutal. COVID-19 created tremendous uncertainty for everyone. We were unsure about almost everything and it created enormous stress. Decisions had to be made quickly and then changed daily and long-term planning became a dart-throwing contest. Amid the uncertainty, I tried to focus on these things:

1. Empathy and constant kindness to the team. Acknowledge that people are scared, exhausted, frustrated, emotional, and that it is OK to feel that way.

2. Being up front about the uncertainty in our decisions. "I don't know if this is the right decision forever, but it's the right decision for today, so we'll try it. If it doesn't work, we'll change again."

3. Focusing on the things I could control. I could not control the vaccine rollout, the lockdown schedule and most of the lost revenue for our business. I could control how I showed up every day and how I communicated with the team, where we spent our money and what we prioritized.

4. Long-term planning. In addition to managing today's crisis, I pushed myself and our team to think about how we'd get out of COVID and what our business needed to look like in future years. It was difficult, people were exhausted and we couldn't always see what tomorrow was going to look like, but we keep going.

Time and money. COVID allowed me to evaluate where we were spending our time and money as a business. I will spend far less time and money on travel moving forward. Flying endlessly around the country for a day of meetings is no longer necessary and a waste of resources. On the flip side, finding important ways to connect in-person to build culture and strategy is vital. On a personal note, I will spend more time with my kids.

Trends can be accelerated. We knew the "shift to digital" was underway and the pandemic accelerated those trends. When you know where the business is going, don't stall getting it there.

Don't put off important work. It's easy to get caught up in today's urgent job and the daily routine. If we've learned anything from COVID, we must focus on what's important, not simply what's in front of us. I will spend far more time getting curious about how we delight our customers three years from now versus how we delighted them yesterday.

THOUGHT #21: AND FINALLY — HAVE FUN!

The best part about being a leader is the opportunity to build and work with a team.

Is there anything more fun in business than being with a group of people you respect, care about and totally gel with? No. When you get the team right, everything else falls into place. The days are filled with interesting discussions and debate, new ideas, a lot of laughs and meaningful, inspiring work.

A winning team finds a way to have fun at work. Teams

who take the time to play together build a deeper level of trust, learn more quickly, are more open to creative solutions and different viewpoints and find more joy in their work. Kindergarten classes spend their day playing to help kids learn. The brain and the heart open to new ideas through play and creativity kicks in.

Show kindness by giving your team permission to find happiness and delight in what they do. Be bold and mandate it, right there beside your business goals. Be loud and proud about it. Be audacious. Set the bar high. Aim to be the "most fun place to work."

Talk to your team. What does joy look like for them? When are they happy at work, what are they doing? What or who makes them laugh or smile? What is their version of fun? What would have to be true to win the most fun at work award? Put all of those things on a board and design your workplace around them.

Then throw a celebration when you hit those best-in-class scores.

Allowing a team to turn their work and workspace into fun is another way to show your kindness as a leader.

Pro-Tip: Here are three quick ideas on how to find some fun at work:

Humour: I do my best to welcome and inject humour into meetings. It feels good to laugh and I find this an effective way to have fun.

Find the fun & games captain: I'm terrible at throwing

parties and celebrations but I love to attend them and know how important it is to have some organized fun at work. Because I'm not a great planner, I delegate this to someone who *loves* this kind of work.

Buy a prop. Our office was in a bit of a rut, so I went out and bought a ping pong table, and we invented Ping Pong Fridays. It's impossible not to have fun when people are playing ping pong. Plus, we weren't sure if we were even allowed to have a ping pong table, so I smuggled it in, making it even more fun to know that we were breaking a small, meaningless rule.

CHAPTER 5:

KINDNESS + THE OUTSIDE WORLD

THOUGHT #22: BE KIND TO THE COMPETITION — THERE'S BOUNTY ENOUGH FOR ALL

I don't much like the competition. I get annoyed when they succeed. I can't stand losing.

But over the years, I've been seeing some gray areas in the winning/losing game.

I've worked hard to train (and convince) myself to get away from the belief that there can only be one winner, that if we come in first, our competition has to lose and vice versa. That kind of thinking is called a scarcity mindset. It's based on the belief there isn't enough to go around, so you better cling to what you have and hold on tight, in fear of losing it all.

Leaders with this mindset tend to focus too heavily on "crushing" the competition and dreaming up ways to "make them lose" instead of spending time focusing on customers.

It's one thing to analyze the market to see what people are responding to but we spend too much time worrying what the other team is doing, who was hired or fired, who's in charge, every little product change they made, their social media and stock performance and on and on. But by doing this, you are wasting your most valuable resource: time. Your competitors' decisions are out of your control and believing you can change their course is not realistic.

The other problem with focusing on the competition? In today's world, you don't have one or two competitors — you are competing with virtually everyone in the business of garnering people's time and attention.

What if you shifted your thinking away from believing there isn't enough to the reality that there's bounty enough for all?

As a fun exercise, spend some time answering this question:

What would happen if you switched your mindset away from "killing the competition" to being kind to your closest competitor? Don't laugh.

What would it do to your strategy?

Would it clear some space to think more deeply about your business or your team?

Would it take undue pressure and stress away from you and your team?

Would it allow you to collaborate with the competing business in ways that could bolster your entire industry?

Ultimately, would it allow you to spend more time and energy super-serving your customers?

Leaders who believe in abundance and kindness will build a growth strategy, one that will deliver a long-lasting positive impact on their business and attract a team of all-stars who are energized and motivated to compete and win in today's marketplace.

It doesn't mean you aren't competing to win, it simply means there *is* bounty enough for all. So, focus on growth and abundance versus market share and scarcity.

Pro-Tip: Kindness to my competitors doesn't come easy, but I have learned that being focused on what others are doing doesn't make me or my business better. Screaming "we're going to crush so and so" is only helpful for about 10 minutes at a staff meeting when people get fired up — but it's not a real strategy because I can't control what another company is going to do. I have spent a lot of time training myself to shift my focus to serving our team and customers. This move didn't come easily to me; I miss the days of screaming and yelling about the competition at staff rallies, but I needed to move to the next level in leadership.

Here's how I think about using kindness with respect to the competition:

Learn from their wins. When a competitor does something well, I like to think about why it was a good idea and how we can learn from it, as opposed to ignoring their victory or being bitter.

Learn from their innovation: Everyone riffs on everyone else's ideas. I pay attention to the market and think about what our team can learn and adopt.

Jealousy is dangerous: Jealousy and envy are destructive. When we are mad at the competition for doing well, we're saying that we're jealous and envious of their position. You don't want to be in this mindset. Find a way to expel this negative energy. Believe me, I'm no less competitive, I just use my energy differently.

THOUGHT #23: KINDNESS IN NEGOTIATION

Every leader needs to be a great negotiator. If you're running a business, you will need to arm wrestle every day of your life, so you better be good and ideally learn to love negotiating.

Being a good negotiator is essential for so many different reasons. It can help you convince someone to see another point of view before making a decision, close a customer or help land a top talent to join your organization, or complete a massive deal that could catapult your business to next-level growth.

Here are the key attributes of a great negotiator:

Outstanding listener. Someone who listens more than talks. Being a good listener allows you to pick up the nuances of a conversation. Don't simply sit and wait for your chance to speak — listen and hear what the other person is saying.

Calm under pressure and capable of keeping emotions in check. Often negotiations go off the rails when you get too close to the deal, it becomes personal and you can't walk away. Stay cool.

A clear thinker. Negotiations can be complex, with many competing agendas, contributing voices and points of view. The ability to think clearly throughout is critical. It is essential to be able to drown out the noise and immaterial information and focus on what's important.

Well prepared. Have a plan (it can be flexible) going into the negotiation, including a realistic goal for closing the deal. If you know roughly what you want beforehand, it will help you see any red flags when the negotiation is getting too far away from what is right for your business.

Kindness. As you get set for your next negotiation, don't forget to bring your kindness superpower along with you. Despite great intentions, leaders often flub negotiations by ignoring the other person's point of view. The ego kicks in and the deal becomes too one-sided. People default to being hard-nosed and spend too much time grinding over trivial details. People who only look out for themselves fail in the long run. You may win a deal through a tough negotiation, but it will backfire over time if it is too one-sided.

Instead of disregarding or ignoring what is essential to the other parties, show kindness and care as much about their position as you do your own. Forget about the win and the glory of getting the deal done and instead put energy into understanding what success looks like for the other side. Here are a few tactics to help you:

Negotiate from the same side of the table. Instead of being on opposite sides of the deal, act like you're on the same team. It's amazing what happens when you work through each other's issues together.

Lead a "whiteboard session" where you write down the reasons why the deal is a good idea and what each side needs to make it work.

Share your financial plan. When you're talking about money, don't be afraid to have an open dialogue about how you're valuing the deal and share as much as you can. We're often too secretive talking about money, yet it's the most crucial part of the negotiation. When both sides better understand what each other wants financially, it helps close the deal.

Be clear about what's important to you. Clearly articulate what's important to you and why. Ensure you get clarity on what they want and need.

Be willing to walk away. It's tough to put a lot of work into something, only to have to shut it down, but if the deal isn't working for both of you, it's OK to walk away.

Pro-Tip: Of the many negotiations I've been involved in, the most rewarding was when we acquired a podcast company. There were three things we did differently that made the process wonderful AND successful:

1. The owner and I handled the deal discussions ourselves. In a big company, usually, negotiations are conducted by the corporate development team and while they were right beside me, I handled the face-to-face conversations. This allowed us to build trust quickly.

2. We both committed from the start that we'd work from the same side of the table. At the founder's suggestion, we read *Getting to Yes* by Roger Fisher and Wiliam Ury to help us stay true to the process.

3. With any negotiation, getting an agreement on what one side is willing to pay versus what the other side wants is always the trickiest part. We decided to share our financial goals to help build trust and transparency, allowing us to get a deal together that worked for both sides.

THOUGHT #24: BE KIND TO YOUR COMMUNITY

Say this out loud: I am in debt to my community. I owe more than gratitude for the land, love and opportunities given to me throughout my lifetime.

We all have a debt to repay. The more you have, the more you owe. It's that simple.

Leaders have a responsibility to build a plan and set a tone for their team and organization. They need to take action in both big and small ways and remember that you can never give too much.

While debt belongs to everyone, it's up to you, the leader, to own the responsibility. You need to rally your team to step up, show kindness and help those who need it most.

Start by defining who your community is and build a kindness plan. How can you use your strength to lift others up? If you are running a local shop, think about how you can help the people who can't afford to shop with you. What about youth who need a break, a mentor or a competitive advantage? What about the hospitals and frontline workers in your neighbourhood? How about a struggling business nearby that isn't as lucky as you? (Yes, every leader gets some luck thrown their way.)

Think about your customer community and what is important to them. Get their feedback. Host town hall meetings and get their input on how you can give back some of the support and money they've given you over the years.

Put your team in the center. Have them make the final decision on where to focus. Recognize not everyone knows how to give back, and some may even see it as an inconvenience. Their body language will say, "I'm too busy to do this." Don't judge them for their resistance, instead get curious about why.

Don't forget to show 1:1 kindness. Think about those who have mentored you along the way. How can you pay it forward? Whose career can you help jumpstart or push along? Which organization would benefit from you being on its board of directors? No one makes it alone in this world and it is your responsibility to lean in and help.

Look inside your organization. Be kind and offer mentorship and sponsorship to up-and-coming internal talent on their leadership journey. It's challenging to navigate a career; you can use your currency to help young, diverse talent get new opportunities by connecting them, coaching them, providing feedback and sponsorship.

Just get going.

> **Pro-Tip:** If you're not sure how to get involved in your community or how to volunteer, start by identifying who you'd like to help. I began my work with Big Brothers, Big Sisters of Toronto because I knew I wanted to help at-risk kids. Once I identified this, I started asking people if they could introduce me to some specialized organizations in this area. LinkedIn is also a great way to source people. After you get some names, set up some meetings to learn about the company, how it works and where you could fit in. It's much easier to get going when you have a general idea of who you want to help.

CHAPTER 6:

KINDNESS + YOU (THE BIG MOMENTS)

THOUGHT #25: THE UGLY STUFF

No matter how much you love being a leader, there are moments where it is genuinely awful. Some days are downright ugly. The pressure from running a team or business or both can be overwhelming. No amount of training can prepare you for the unexpected crises that fall in your lap.

Financial challenges are constant — there is always a need to make more money. Everyone wants more, including the employees, shareholders, owners and customers. Personnel issues are unforgiving and relentless — someone is always unhappy and on the verge of quitting, being poached or needs to be fired. And, sadly, you will even be faced with sickness and death of employees. Toss in competitive battles, disruption and the occasional sale or takeover, and some days you wonder which way is up.

This is the ugly stuff no one warns you about before you take the job. When things get ugly and the pressure heats up, you need to know how to manage the stress. If you can't manage stress as a leader, you won't be effective, the job will weigh you down and stop being fun, and you'll eventually burn out.

The tricky thing about stress is it has a way of sneaking up on you, and you must learn to be self-aware and catch it early before it blows up. Pay attention to your body as the signs often come out in a physical way. You may be suffering from headaches, a lack of energy or tiredness, or have frequent colds or an upset stomach.

Stress can also cause anxiety and panic attacks with a sudden shortness of breath, a racing heart, tingling in fingers and a feeling of a loss of control.

Or maybe stress makes you sad or irritable or pushes you to indulge in food or alcohol or drugs.

Whatever it is, you're not alone. Every leader goes through this and your #1 priority, before you do anything else, is to be kind to yourself. This is especially true for people-pleasers who put everyone else first.

Practice daily self-care and develop a routine that will proactively help you manage stress. It's not exciting, and it requires incredible self-discipline, but if you can maintain a healthy diet, exercise and get enough sleep at night, you will build a great foundation to help you fight off stress. Then ask yourself what else do you need beside the foundation to get through the tough times? Friends? Family? A hobby? Travel?

Take your vacation. It's likely, and OK, that you work more than 40 hours a week, however, working 24/7, 365 is not helpful or necessary. Set some work boundaries to ensure you find time to recoup and recover. Our bodies and minds need to rest.

Have a safe network. Whether it's a confidant, a therapist, a mentor or all of the above, make sure you're surrounded by people who can help you when you are struggling or need someone to talk to. It's important that this person will keep what you say confidential.

Develop an emergency plan. Even with the best routine in the world, you're going to be overwhelmed at times and in these moments you will need to a) recognize it is happening and b) have a mechanism that helps you get through challenging moments. This can be deep breathing or meditation, getting outside for a run, walk or ride, playing a sport, shutting off the phone and going out with friends, or maybe it's simply going to bed!

There is no right and wrong, it's just about finding what works for you.

Pro-Tip: Stress has a way of sneaking up on me and I still from time to time have what I think would be diagnosed as panic attacks. My heart starts racing, I start to worry and quickly get panicky. It's a confusing feeling as my brain is wired to be happy, optimistic and positive, yet, on the other hand, my body is saying "not so fast".

Over time, I have become much better at recognizing and managing my stress. Here's what I do to cope and practice self-care:

Call out my anxiety. It's not as scary when you know what's happening and you can give it a name. My kids and husband know to ask, "Are you having a panic attack?" Once

I acknowledge what's going on, I know what I need to do to calm myself down.

Exercise. Exercise. Exercise. I work out early each weekday morning. I walk my dog, swim, play tennis, paddleboard, and generally do whatever I can to burn off steam. I have an excess amount of energy that I need to burn off to help me take care of my mental health.

Laugh. I laugh a lot. I love the people I work with – they make me laugh every day, and I have a close circle of friends and family. I need to be around good people.

Practice gratitude. I practice gratitude. I know I have a great life, and I am truly grateful for everything I have.

Watch baseball. I'm a baseball nerd, and watching baseball is good for my soul.

My mental health struggles have influenced my approach to leadership. As a leader, I do my very best to create a kind environment where people can be their true selves. We are all human, which means we are not perfect. Too often, I think people are aiming for perfection, and it is simply not attainable.

I encourage our team to put their hands up if they need help, reminding them I have their back. Not only is it OK to ask for help, but it's the best thing you can do for yourself.

THOUGHT #26 – MANAGING ANGER

Is it possible to be a kind leader and get angry?
Of course.

Not only is it possible, but it is necessary and completely acceptable.

Things go wrong — competitors win, mistakes happen, products fail, people do awful things, and pandemics happen! It's natural and healthy to get angry at times, and if you don't, you have either become complacent or are burying your emotions. Neither works.

I don't know any winning leader who doesn't get frustrated and mad when they lose. No competitor accepts defeat with a shrug of the shoulders. If losing has become acceptable to you, it's time for you to make a change. Remember, your team takes their cues from you, and if you are indifferent about outcomes, everyone else will eventually turn down their competitive spark and become complacent too. When mediocrity sets in, top talent will leave to join a team that wants to win.

If complacency isn't your issue, you need to learn how to manage anger. What do you do when things go south and you're furious?

Get mad and use kindness!

That may sound ridiculous, but you can channel your anger in a productive way when you lead with kindness. Instead of raging at everyone and everything when something goes wrong, lean in and go hard on the issue but be soft on the people.

Get curious with the team and stay calm. What happened? How are they feeling? Are they beating themselves up? Are they owning the issue or deflecting it? Are they looking for solutions or pointing fingers? After you've done your assessment, you can determine whether this group needs you to push them harder, wrap your arms around them, or both.

For the people who take ownership, you will need to

provide support and coaching, and for those who deflect the blame, you will need to step in and push accountability. To be a great leader, you must shift your approach depending on what the team needs. So many leaders get this wrong, applying the same process to everyone. When you have a kindness frame of mind, it is easier to think about how you can be most helpful in service to the team.

In either situation, get your frustrations out into the open. Having difficult conversations is essential to building a robust and open culture. If you handle losing productively, you can learn and improve.

If it was your error, OWN IT. Stand up in front of your team, call it out and get mad at yourself. One of the most powerful things you can do as a leader is admit when you are wrong. It gives everyone else permission to do the same.

The key is to not mistake kindness with emotionlessness or complacency.

If you're mad, get mad. Expressing anger is very healthy when done right.

Pro Tip #1: Managing my anger I spent a year with brutal back pain that threw me off balance. I had no specific injury or cause for the pain, it just happened and wouldn't go away. The pain shut down most of my daily exercise, which was frustrating and made it hard to manage stress. After several visits with doctors and a back surgeon, and a ton of reading, I now believe my pain was caused from emotional stress. I had a lot inside that I was pushing through, including a new job, a very ill mom, the recent loss of my dad, and a young family. There are many people that believe that suppressing emotion, especially anger, will cause you physical pain. The point? We all carry stress in different ways, and for me, it hit me in the back. Once I accepted it was stress related and worked through my emotions, the pain went away and hasn't returned. For more on this theory, you can read *Healing Back Pain* by Dr. John Sarno.

Pro Tip #2: Managing someone else's anger When you are on the receiving end of an unreasonable customer complaint or an angry co-worker, it's natural and easy to want to give it back to them. They are being mean and unfair, and you get defensive, tempers flare, tensions rise and the next thing you know, you are volleying passive aggressive insults, or you're in a full-blown argument. Or maybe you are the type to shut down during confrontation and instead of responding to an angry note or comment, you ignore it, hit delete and walk away.

Both responses are natural. Neither are wrong. Sometimes an angry coworker or client turns out to be a bully and they need to be barked at. Sometimes stepping away is the perfect response. The only problem with these approaches is they usually leave you feeling crappy. Either you're frustrated that you lost your temper or you're resentful that you didn't say your piece.

There's a third, under-used and very satisfying option you can choose. Try kindness.

Using kindness to counter someone else's pointless

rant can be a fun way to defuse a situation and stand your ground. Treat it like a game. The jerkier you are with me, the nicer I'll be to you. The person on the other side is often left confused and feels terrible that they've just railed on someone as nice as you.

The next time someone sends you an unfair, unwarranted and mean "you suck" message (this often happens in my business), write a friendly response back instead of ignoring it.

Something like this:

"Dear X,

Thank you so much for taking the time to send in your thoughts on my performance. I was born and raised in Toronto and am the youngest of six kids. I followed my passion and dreams to work in the media and am so grateful to have a job in service of loyal and wonderful customers like yourself."

Make sure you personalize the note to ensure cranky pants is clear it wasn't a mistake.

Hit send and imagine what happens when they open the email and instead of getting a cranky note back, they get a personalized, lovely note of gratitude.

Kindness works in person too. When someone tears a strip off of you, instead of arguing, give them every ounce of kindness and compassion you have. Thank them for the feedback. Ask them how you can help and what they'd like you to do about it. Put the solution back on them. Get creative and once again, treat it like a game and see how fast you can turn the situation from hostile to happy.

This approach may seem childish or a waste of time, but it's not. Confrontation and hostility are brutal on your mental health. Using kindness to get out of the situation allows you to stand your ground, take control and power back from the other person and ultimately come out a winner without having to get into a full-blown shouting match.

THOUGHT #27: THE JOURNEY

Becoming a great leader is a never-ending journey. You can't check off a box on a to-do list because the work is never complete. The only way to survive, thrive and have fun is to understand it is a long game with no final inning.

It may be scary to think you will never complete the "task". We are more comfortable knowing what we are working towards and what the path is to get there. Most of us like maps with clear directions and don't like getting lost or wasting time stumbling around in the wrong place, unsure where we're going.

Businesses and people don't come with maps or straight lines. They are imperfect. What works in one situation won't work in another. Change is constant and things evolve. Even if you've learned to "master" something — there will ALWAYS be a disruptive new idea that comes along, and you'll have to adapt.

As a leader, you need to get comfortable with imperfection, accept the journey and understand you will take many steps forward only to hit a roadblock that sets you back. You must be kind to yourself along the way, forgive missteps and celebrate your growth. Be humble and curious and accept that you don't know everything.

Perhaps the most important (and sometimes hardest) part of the journey will be the day you step aside and hand over the reins to a successor. People often find themselves in a position where they aren't ready to walk away; next-level leaders instead spend their careers dedicated to building emerging stars.

Succession planning is the ultimate act of kindness. If your mission is to lead with kindness, identifying, coaching and growing, a replacement should be a focus, and when the time is right, you should be keen to "get out of the way" for the next in line. Succession planning is not about you — it is in service of the business and the team.

The faster you accept that leadership is a journey, the easier it will be for you to enjoy the ride and continuously move on to your next new adventure. Moments may come to an end, but the ride doesn't.

Pro-Tip: Here is how I have approached my journey:

Build an extensive network. My career has been narrow, and it is critical I maintain a large peer group to help open my mind to new ways of thinking and partnerships.

Build a tight, trusted network. Knowing many people is wise, but you can't trust everyone. You need a small group to get unbiased input, advice and coaching along the way.

Adopt the mindset "This won't last forever." Call it out as a positive, not a negative. "This won't last forever because I will do something interesting next" is better than "this won't last forever, and I'll lose my house, car and dog!" Change is scary *and* a good thing.

Take joy in other people succeeding. If scrolling through social media and seeing other people succeed makes you jealous, get to the bottom of why. Jealousy is not helpful on the journey.

Have a side hustle and outside interests. They don't need to make you money, although if they can, great, but it will give you a purpose outside of your day-to-day work and help you think about what's next. Plus, it's fun.

Learn how to save your money. I'm not independently wealthy and have a mortgage, humans and pets I'm responsible for. The most stressful part of something coming to an end is losing the income. It's critical that you start saving money as early as possible in your career. Manage what you earn and build up your savings. It's also vital that you understand any company programs available to you, like stock matching incentives or pension plans. I encourage you to think about money as a tool, more so than a status symbol. Take the time to learn how investing and saving works. Don't put it off.

Love to learn and accept that you don't know anything. Everything is a journey and you'll learn along the way. The unhappiest people I know are the ones who think they know or need to know everything. The need to be the smartest person in the room is stressful and unnecessary. Accept you don't know everything. Ask questions, be curious and learn. It's fun.

Lean on your kindness superpower. Be kind to yourself, others and the journey.

Control your destiny. I've been lucky to work for an incredible company for over 20 years. I have stayed because I enjoy the work and the people. The company presumably kept me because they have found value in having me as an employee. I accept that I am only in control of my decisions, not theirs. I focus on working hard, being curious, learning new skills, developing and recruiting an all-star team and building my succession plan. I do my best to lead with kindness, creativity, integrity and fun and it's up to everyone else to determine what they think of me. That's none of my business. I like to say to my bosses — I have enough decisions to make, what you do with me isn't my problem!

MY FINAL THOUGHT #28:
IT'S ALL ABOUT THE END GAME

It's your career.

What you do, how you do it and who you do it with is up to you.

You are the boss of yourself. Some people will have some authority over you, whether they hire or promote or fire you, and some situations will arise that are totally out of your hands. But ultimately, to succeed, you must have the belief that you control your destiny. Your path is yours alone and doesn't have to look like someone else's.

If you love what you do, keep doing it.

If you're bored or unhappy, make a change.

If you dream of something new, make it happen.

When faced with significant decisions, I fast forward to the end of my life or career. I imagine if I will be happy with the choice I'm about to make — if I am, I do it; if I'm not, I don't.

I live in fear of these five words: "I wish I would have," and they guide my choices.

That's why I wrote this book and why I'm focused on kindness.

Because when it's all over, I hope people will say, "Julie wasn't perfect, but she sure was kind."

Imperfectly kind.

CREDITS

The following materials were referenced:

Thought #2: Dan Harris quote in reference to the original name for his book *10 Percent Happier*.

Thought #4: Diversity Is Good for Business, University of Waterloo website: https://uwaterloo.ca/news/global-impact/diversity-good-business.

Thought #9: The Magic Relationship Ratio, According To Science, The Gottman Institute website: https://www.gottman.com/blog/the-magic-relationship-ratio-according-science/

Thought #23: Roger Fisher & William Ury, *Getting to Yes*, 3rd edition (New York: 2011).

Thought #26: Dr. John Sarno, *Healing Back Pain: The Mind-Body Connection,* (New York: Grand Central Publishing 1991).

Thank you to the following people for your contributions:

Thought #1: Candice Faktor, for your beautiful coaching.

Thought #3: Cathy Mobilos, for being a wonderful teacher.

Thought #3: Chuck McCoy (boss) for your never-ending guidance, wisdom and mentorship.

Thought #9: Andrew Sutherland (colleague) for your often used "feedback is a gift" mantra.

Thought #13: Erin Davis (morning host) for coming back, saving the day and bringing Cooper with you! Credit goes to you for always being quick to say "there's bounty enough for all" too in Thought #22.

Thought #13: Pat Bohn for your "ditch" analogy.

Thought #23: Steve Pratt (owner) and Pacific Content (podcast company) for your partnership.

Thought #24: Big Brothers, Big Sisters of Toronto is an outstanding not-for-profit organization that creates individual and group mentoring relationships amongst adults and youth.

WITH THANKS & GRATITUDE

To my editor and advisor on this project — Paul Fraumeni. Without your help, input, encouragement and hands-on editing, this book wouldn't have happened. Paul has a side hustle as my brother. Thank you for being good at that too.

To my designer Dania Zafar for your wonderful layout and cover work.

To Kristin Hatcher and the Writing in Community members and coaches for your support, guidance, feedback and inspiration.

To my colleagues, managers and teammates (past and present). Working with you is a privilege, you make me better and fill my days with joy and laughter. This book is a collection of the many things I've learned from you along the way. I am forever indebted. Thank you, Jordan Banks, Andrea Goldstein and Tony Cimino for your professional and personal support on this journey.

To my employer, Rogers Communications, for giving me the greatest gift you can give an employee. Space and freedom to be myself, a wealth of opportunities, wonderful problems and challenges to solve, a team of all-stars to work with, infinite fun, personal care and a north star to shoot for. I am forever grateful.

To my large family. My in-laws Marnie, Jim & Terry Adam. My parents, Mary & Jack Fraumeni, for raising me to believe in myself and stay true to my values. My dad was my original mentor and the first person I saw demonstrate kindness in leadership. He encouraged me to be fiercely independent, to follow my interests and to celebrate my relentless drive, curiosity and ambition. He also taught me how to score a ballgame. My incredible sisters who helped raise me — Mary Ellen, Martha, Ammey — the one who gave me the gentle push and direction to get my act together after high school and of course Angie, our superhero. To my eleven nieces and nephews — Glenna, Nick, Sam, Rich, Matt, Benny, Emily, Tommy, Sarah, Michael & Jadyn — for always letting me sit at the kids table, where life is more fun!

To my high school BFFs: I'm lucky to have your daily messages and support — Janet, Jennie, Laura, Renee and Sarah Superville McComb — you'll always be our Supergirl and our queen of kindness. Special thanks to Cathy Mobilos, who doubled as my proof-reader and Lexie Badali for your input on this project and for rescuing me in grade 9.

Finally, to the three most important people in my life. My boys, Jack and Cal — you can be whatever you want to be, so go for it and be kind along the way. I've got your back. Darren — you've been my everything for twenty-five+ years – every time I tried to quit this book, you gave me a reason to keep going, so I did. Your support is endless. With love, thanks and gratitude. I'm a lucky girl.

And, of course — Phoebe the dog.

Made in United States
Orlando, FL
08 March 2022

15529626R00062